WORSHIP
According to the WORD

An Introduction to the Regulative Principle of Worship

Michael C. Griggs

5thKingdomMinistries.com

Copyright © 2019 Michael C. Griggs

5th Kingdom Ministries
5thKingdomMinistries.com

Booklet Design by Justin Turley

ISBN 978-1-797736-11-2

All scripture taken from the New King James Version®.
Copyright © 1982 by Thomas Nelson, Inc.
Used by permission.

*"Those that truly love God will make it their
constant care and endeavour to keep His commandments,
particularly those that relate to His worship."*
—Matthew Henry (1662-1714)

*"...all worshiping, honouring, or service invented
by the brain of man in the religion of God,
without His own express commandment, is idolatry."*
—John Knox (1515-1572)

TABLE OF CONTENTS

Introduction 7

Chapter 1
A Bit of History 11

Chapter 2
Biblical Principles 19

Chapter 3
The Passages 23

Chapter 4
New Testament Considerations & Applications 31

Appendix
Regulative Principle for All of Life? 43

INTRODUCTION

There are many different debates taking place in the church today. For example: Is our salvation determined by God's predestined plan, or by our making a decision to follow Christ? Are all the spiritual gifts still in operation today, or only some? Are the Old Testament promises to the Jews fulfilled by the church, or by the modern nation of Israel?

All of these are important debates, but there is another debate that I believe also needs to happen. To some extent, this debate is already taking place in the church, but it doesn't receive the attention it deserves. I'm referring to the debate about how strictly the Bible regulates our corporate worship. Or, to put it in more technical terms, the debate over the normative principle of worship vs. the regulative principle of worship.

The normative principle could be described in the following (oversimplified) way: In worship, we may do whatever God has not forbidden. In other words, if God's word hasn't told us that we may not do something, then we are free to do that thing. For instance, the Bible doesn't forbid us from juggling in a worship service, therefore, it would be acceptable to juggle in worship (Of course, I don't mean to imply that those who hold to the normative principle juggle in their worship services, I'm only using juggling as an illustration).

On the other hand we have the regulative principle, which could be described as: In worship, we may only do those things which God has commanded us to do. Again using the juggling illustration, since God has not told us in His word to juggle in worship, then we may not juggle in our services.

In this booklet, I'll be making a case for the regulative principle. To do this, I want to look at some history, some general principles from Scripture, and, more importantly, some passages that support the regulative principle. The focus of this booklet will be on what we *do* in a *corporate worship service*. There are other important aspects of worship that won't be covered in this booklet, such as:

1. All of life as worship. In one sense, everything we do, if done in accordance with God's word, is worship. Even mundane tasks should be done to the glory of God (1 Cor. 10:31).

2. Our heart attitude in worship. It is possible to worship God in a way that is technically correct, and yet still

isn't pleasing to Him. Even if every aspect of our worship is as close to the biblical ideal as humanly possible, we will fall short of true worship if our hearts are cold, or worse, unregenerate (not born again).

3. The relationship between biblical justice and worship. God is very concerned with how we worship corporately, but He is also very concerned with the condition of society. In fact, when God's people are not seeking justice (biblically defined) in society, God says He *hates* their corporate worship (Isa. 1:11-17; Amos 5:21-24; etc.).

These aspects of worship are important and should not be ignored. Our focus for now, however, is on what we should be doing when we meet on the Lord's day to worship with other Christians. I believe the Bible teaches that we should only do what God has told us to do. No less, and no more.

Chapter 1

A BIT OF HISTORY

If you want to make a case for a particular belief, especially one that isn't common in your day, it will greatly help your cause if you can show that Christians in other centuries held to that belief as well. While you won't find the term "regulative principle" until more recently, the idea does go back centuries. In this chapter, we'll be looking particularly at the time of the Reformation (1500's A.D.) onward. While the idea of the regulative principle can be found prior to the Reformation, the regulative principle was one of the areas of contention between the Protestants and the Roman Catholic Church. So, being a Protestant, I would like to begin at that time period.

The Reformation is rightly known as the time when the church recovered the doctrine of justification by faith alone.

But the real issue at the center of debate was the authority of the Scriptures. While the Roman Catholic Church would say that the Bible was *an* authority, the Reformers believed that the Bible was *the* authority. They believed it was the authority by which every belief and practice should be measured. "Every practice" would, of course, include how God was to be worshiped.

After the Reformers, there arose a group in England known as the Puritans. These Puritans took the teachings of the Reformers and refined them even further. The name "Puritan" was first used as a nickname (and not a friendly one) for those who wanted to reform, or purify, the Church of England. Later, the name came to be used for others who held to a "puritanical" type of Christianity. In 1677, a group of puritanical Baptists wrote a statement of faith that was officially adopted in 1689. This statement is known as the London Baptist Confession of Faith, and it is one of, if not the most important documents in Baptist history. It is to the LBCF that we now turn to help us better understand what the regulative principle is. The LBCF doesn't use the term "regulative principle," but the concept is still there.

The LBCF begins by affirming that the Scriptures are all we need for understanding how God wants to be worshiped. In fact, it says that "The Holy Scripture is the *only* sufficient, certain, and infallible rule of all saving knowledge, faith, and obedience..." (chapter 1; paragraph 1; emphasis mine).

It goes on to say that "The whole counsel of God concerning all things necessary for His own glory, man's salvation, faith, and life, is either expressly set down or necessarily contained in the Holy Scripture: unto which *nothing at any time is to be added*, whether by new revelation of the Spirit, or *traditions of men.*" (chap. 1; par. 6; emphasis mine).

The idea of adding to the Scripture is not referring to gluing extra pages into your Bible and calling them Scripture. Not adding to Scripture means not devising new doctrines or practices that are not derived from the word of God. This is especially important concerning worship: "...the acceptable way of worshipping the true God, is instituted by Himself, and so limited by His own revealed will, that *He may not be worshipped according to the imagination and devices of men,...or any other way not prescribed in the Holy Scriptures.*" (chap. 22; par. 1; emphasis mine).

To put it in a more modern paraphrase: "You may not worship God in ways that were invented by humans. You may only do what God has told you to do in the Bible." At this point, some would object to the regulative principle by pointing out that since God's word doesn't give us every minute detail of what should go on in a worship service, we *have to* do things that aren't in the Bible! The LBCF deals with this issue as well. After stating that we are not allowed to add any traditions of men to our worship, the confession says:

> "*Nevertheless, we acknowledge...that there are some circumstances concerning the worship of God...which are to be ordered by the light of nature and Christian prudence, according to the general rules of the Word..." (chap. 1; par. 6).*

Again, let me paraphrase: "There are some *aspects*

(circumstances) of worship that can be done according to what we think best. But even in those things, we are still to consider biblical principles."

So, when it comes to certain *circumstances* that pertain to worship, like: how many songs should be sung, what time the service should be held, how long the service should last, etc.—when it comes to these types of issues, God has left them up to us to decide. However, when it comes to what are commonly called the *elements* of worship (prayer, singing, preaching, etc.), we may only do what God has told us to do. No less, and no more. This is what Baptists used to believe.

The regulative principle, however, was not invented by Baptists. As stated earlier, the idea was common during the Reformation of the 1500's. This is not to say that every Reformer held to the regulative principle. In fact, the views of the most famous Reformer, Martin Luther, would be considered more in line with the normative principle of worship, though I don't think he'd approve of some of the things that take place in modern worship services.

Many other Reformers, however, did hold to the regulative principle. John Calvin, who is probably the next best known Reformer, said this about the 2nd commandment:

> *"[W]hen it is a matter of worshipping God, we are not to give any attention whatever to our own imagination. But we are to follow in all simplicity what He has ordained in His Word, without adding anything to it at all."*[1]

---

[1] Joe Morecraft, III, *How God Wants Us to Worship Him: A Defense of the Bible as the Only Standard For Modern Worship* (San Antonio, TX: The Vision Forum, Inc., 2004), p. 83

Chapter 1: A Bit of History

In one weeklong dispute between Roman Catholics and Protestants (Oct. 1st-8th, 1536, in Lausanne, Switzerland), ten issues were to be debated publicly. These ten issues (called "conclusions") were written down by the Reformer William Farel (1489-1565). A summary of the 7th conclusion states:

> *"The [Protestant] Church rejects all manner of worship of God save that which is spiritual and ordained by the Word of God."*[2]

A lesser-known, yet highly important Reformer, Pierre Viret (1511-1571), says this in his book on the basics of the Christian faith:

> *"[God] does not wish to be served according to the will and imagination of man, but according to His own will...This is why He has universally forbidden all men...to 'add unto the word which I command you...'"*[3]

No discussion of Reformers and the regulative principle would be complete without mentioning John Knox (1515-1572). John Knox, whose views on resisting ungodly governments can be found in America's Declaration of Independence, once said:

---

[2] R. A. Sheats, *Pierre Viret: The Angel of the Reformation* (Tallahassee, FL: Zurich Publishing, 2012), p.58

[3] Pierre Viret, *Simple Exposition of the Principle Points of the Christian Faith*, Trans. R. A. Sheats (Tallahassee, FL: Zurich Publishing, 2013), p. 9. Note: the copy I have is no longer in print. This book is now available under a new title: *A Simple Exposition of the Christian Faith*

> "...all worshiping, honouring, or service invented by the brain of man in the religion of God, without His own express commandment, is idolatry."[4]

As we move from the Reformers of the 1500's to the Puritans of the 1600's, we see many (though not all) Protestants holding to the regulative principle. We have already seen what the English Baptists believed by what they wrote in the LBCF. I chose to look at the LBCF because I am a Baptist. However, on the topic of worship, the Baptist confession is virtually word for word in agreement with the Westminster Confession (Presbyterian; 1647) and the Savoy Declaration (Congregationalist; 1658).

When these English Protestants began migrating to America, they brought their regulative principle views with them. In fact, one of the primary reasons they came to America was so that they could worship free from human inventions. They wanted "a pure worship, unalloyed by merely human traditions without biblical mandate; this was a major reason for leaving England for New England..."[5]

While many European Protestants came to America, some who stayed behind would suffer greatly for their regulative principle views.

> "From 1660 to 1688 in Scotland, over 18,000 Presbyterian

---

[4] Quoted in: Douglas Wilson, *For Kirk and Covenant: The Stalwart Courage of John Knox* (Nashville, TN: Cumberland House, 2000), p. 39

[5] Horton Davies, *The Worship of the American Puritans* (Morgan, PA: Soli Deo Gloria Publications, 1999), p. x

men, women and children—whole families and congregations—were brutally tortured and murdered at the hands of the bloody Stuart kings for one reason: they would not submit to the king's liturgies and inventions in their worship services. They would not give up the regulative principle of worship!"[6]

In the following century (1700's), the regulative principle was again a widely held view. Some of the more popular Bible commentaries from that era, like Matthew Henry (Presbyterian) and John Gill (Baptist) taught the regulative principle. And when American Baptists began writing their own confessions, they left the regulative principle ideas intact. The wording of the Philadelphia (1742) and Charleston (1767) confessions of faith is exactly the same as the LBCF in those paragraphs that were quoted earlier (chap. 1, par. 1; chap. 1, par. 6; chap. 22, par. 1). As you can see, the regulative principle has a rich history amongst European and American Protestants.

---

6 Joe Morecraft, III, *How God Wants Us to Worship Him*, p. 39

Chapter 2

BIBLICAL PRINCIPLES

Before we get into specific passages that support the regulative principle, it may be helpful to look at some general principles that would suggest having a regulative principle mindset.

First, the sufficiency of Scripture. Many modern evangelicals claim to believe in the sufficiency of Scripture, but very few actually do. Paul, however, clearly said that Scripture is what makes us "complete, thoroughly equipped for every good work." (2 Tim. 3:16-17). Worship is a good work, and the Bible thoroughly equips us to do it. It doesn't halfway equip us, and it doesn't kinda-sorta equip us; it *thoroughly* equips us.

To add extra-biblical elements of worship to our services is a denial of the sufficiency of Scripture. To say on one hand that the Bible is sufficient—and then to say that we *must* add things that aren't in the Bible in order to *really* worship God—is a contradiction.

Second, the only way to be sure your worship is pleasing to God, is to do only what the Bible says to do. If God has told you in His word to do something, then you can be certain that it will please Him. If He forbids you to do something, then you know that doing that thing will not please Him. But when we add to worship those things that are neither commanded nor forbidden, we can only guess as to whether or not God likes what we are doing, but we can't be certain.

We might say that a particular thing makes us feel closer to God, but our feelings aren't always correct. Some may argue that God has told them to do something that isn't in Scripture. But how do you know that it was God who "spoke" to you? Satan likes giving instructions for worship too (Deut. 32:16-17; 1 Cor. 10:20). If he tried to deceive the Son of God in the area of worship (Matt. 4:8-9), do you really think he won't try to deceive others? Instead of basing your view of worship on what you feel God has told *you*, base your views on what God has told *everyone* (in His word).

Third, if God's word spelled out, in detail, everything that was not to be done in worship, the Bible would be a mile thick. There are a million things that we could come up with that aren't specifically forbidden in a worship service. God never told us not to jump rope, play cards, have push-up contests, etc., in our worship services. If God did prohibit these things (and much more) in His word, it would be so thick that no one would read it. So, instead, He simply told us what *to* do.

Fourth, the detail of worship in the tabernacle/temple. When God was bringing His people into the promised land, He gave them instructions on worship. From those instructions we see that God is picky about how He is to be worshiped. God's attitude was not "I don't care how you all worship Me, just so long as your heart is in the right place." For several chapters (Ex. 25-31), God gives Moses detailed instructions on what the tabernacle would look like, how offerings were to be made, and even what the priests were to wear.

While these instructions are no longer binding under the new covenant, they do show that God doesn't leave it up to us to figure out how to worship Him. These laws also show that we don't have a lot of freedom to do what we want in worship. When it comes to the circumstances surrounding worship we do have some freedom, but when it comes to the main parts (elements) of worship, we are not free to do whatever we think best. God didn't give Moses the right to make up new ways of worship. He doesn't give us that right either.

Fifth, our hearts and minds are corrupt. In Mark 7, Jesus condemns the church leaders of His day for holding to extra-biblical traditions (vv. 6-13). Although the main issue wasn't corporate worship, the attitude that Jesus was condemning often corrupts our worship as well (v. 7). The problem was that the Pharisees thought the inventions of men were just as good, godly, and edifying as the commands of God. But this can never be the case! Anything that comes from the mind and heart of God will always be good because He is good.

But any worship that comes from the mind and heart of man is suspect because the heart and mind of every human is corrupted by sin (vv. 21-22). True worship is that which comes from the mind of God. Anything else is tainted by our depravity.

Chapter 3

THE PASSAGES

And now we come to the most important arguments for the regulative principle. History is important. General principles, if they are derived from God's word, do give us much guidance. But the best evidence for the regulative principle of worship is found in the passages that either imply or clearly state that, in worship, we may only do what God has told us to do. It is to those passages that we now turn.

Genesis 4:1-7

Often, the first few chapters of Genesis contain allusions to major Bible themes that are more fully developed as God's word unfolds. For instance, the idea of marriage is found in Gen. 1:27-28 and 2:22-24, even though very little detail is given. As we go through the rest of the Bible, we learn much more about marriage. The coming of Christ is also alluded to in chapter 3, verse 15, but you won't understand much about the Messiah until you read more of the Bible. Since how we worship is such an important issue, shouldn't we expect to see it discussed in the first few chapters of our Bibles? We should, and indeed, we do.

In Gen. 4, Cain brings an offering of "the fruit of the ground" to God (v. 3). Cain's brother Abel, also brings an offering. But Abel offers sheep as a sacrifice (vv. 2, 4). God was pleased with Abel's offering but He wasn't pleased with Cain's (vv. 4-5). There are many opinions as to why God didn't accept Cain's offering, and while Cain's heart attitude was likely a factor, God said that Cain didn't "*do* well" (v. 7). It is difficult to say with certainty what Cain did, or didn't do, that was the reason for his offering being rejected. We have no recorded commands at this point pertaining to offering sacrifices.

We do have, however, a clue as to how God wanted to be worshiped. In Gen. 3:21, God made coverings from the skin of an animal to cover Adam and Eve's shame. Because they sinned, an animal had to be sacrificed by God. Abel's offering was according to the pattern of the first sacrifice; Cain's was not. Abel followed God's example, and Cain, it appears, thought that he could determine what to offer to God.

Of course, this passage alone does not prove the regulative principle, but it implies that when God gives instruction (by command or example) we may not deviate from it. It also shows that God doesn't accept all types of worship that we may choose to offer. As with many themes in Scripture, the principles of worship are only vaguely alluded to in the first few chapters of Genesis, but are stated more clearly later on.

Exodus 20:4-6; Deuteronomy 5:8-10

These verses contain the 2nd of the Ten Commandments. As with the first passage we looked at, I will freely admit that the regulative principle cannot be proven from these passages either. So in order to know why I included them, we must first look at what the Ten Commandments are, and what the 2nd commandment is teaching.

The Ten Commandments are a summary of all the other commands in Scripture. For example, all the regulations in God's word dealing with sexual sins are summarized in the command "You shall not commit adultery." Likewise, we would expect that all of the many commands in Scripture dealing with how to worship would be summarized in one of the Ten Commandments as well. The 2nd commandment is the summary of those commands.

On the surface, it may seem like the 1st and 2nd commandments are saying the same thing. The 1st commandment says, basically: "Don't worship other gods." The 2nd says: "Don't worship idols." But God wasn't stuttering, they are different. The 1st commandment is dealing with *who* we worship: God alone. The 2nd is dealing with *how* we worship: in God's way alone.[7] So if other texts

---

[7] For a more detailed explanation about the differences between the 1st and 2nd commandments, see my article on this subject at: 5thKingdomMinistries.com/what-is-the-difference-between-the-first-and-second-commandment

of Scripture teach the regulative principle, then those texts would all fall under the umbrella of the 2nd commandment.

Lest you think that I'm making up these ideas, look at what the Puritan Matthew Henry has to say in his commentary on Exodus 20. Regarding the difference between the 1st and 2nd commandments, Henry says:

> *"The first commandment concerns the object of our worship, Jehovah, and Him only....The second commandment concerns the ordinances of worship, or the way in which God will be worshiped..."*

Matthew Henry also believed that the 2nd commandment was a summary of all the other commands (ordinances) that pertained to worship:

> *"[T]he second commandment, though, in the letter of it, it is only a prohibition of false worships, yet includes a precept of worshipping God in all those ordinances which He has instituted."*

The 2nd commandment also states that God is a jealous God. When Henry comments on this, his regulative principle tendencies can be seen. He says that "If God is jealous...", then we ought to be "afraid of offering any worship to God otherwise than as He has appointed in His word." In other words, we should be afraid to worship in ways that aren't in the Bible.

But where did Matthew Henry get this idea that we should be scared to worship in ways that God hasn't commanded us to? Does the Bible teach this? It does, as our next passage clearly shows.

Leviticus 10:1-3

This passage is the locus classicus (classic example) for the regulative principle. The very first time that the Levitical priests offered sacrifices to God, Aaron's sons Nadab and Abihu were serving as priests. They decided to offer some sort of "strange fire before the LORD." Just for doing that, God killed them. What was Nadab and Abihu's crime? What was so bad about offering this fire?

Many opinions have been given about what this fire was and why it was so offensive to God. The text, however, doesn't tell us what the nature of this fire was, but it does tell us why God was angry. Nadab and Abihu worshiped God in a way "which He had not commanded them." (v. 1). Their sin was that they innovated, they invented a new thing in the worship of God. God had given them detailed commands regulating how He was to be worshiped, but Aaron's sons chose to add something to worship that God had not told them to do. In doing so, they were not regarding God as holy, nor were they glorifying Him (v. 3). Doing things in worship which God has not commanded is dangerous.

When the Pilgrims came to America in 1620, they brought with them the Geneva Bible (instead of the King James version). The study notes in the Geneva Bible give us insight into the views and beliefs of our Pilgrim forefathers. Commenting on Lev. 10:3, the Geneva Bible says (speaking from God's perspective): "I will punish them that serve Me otherwise than I have commanded…"

Matthew Henry, in his commentary on this passage says:

"...it is called strange fire; and, though not expressly forbidden, it was crime enough that God commanded it not. For (as bishop Hall well observes here) 'It is a dangerous thing, in the service of God, to decline [deviate] from His own institutions...'" Henry continues: "...being a holy God, and a sovereign Lord, He must always be worshipped with holiness and reverence, and exactly according to His own appointment..."

Another Englishman, Matthew Poole (1624-1679) writes in his commentary (English Annotations on the Holy Bible):

> *"...seeing Moses himself neither did nor might do any thing in God's worship without God's command, which is oft noted of him, for these [Nadab & Abihu] to do it was a more unpardonable and inexcusable presumption."*

English Baptist John Gill (1697-1771), in his *Exposition of the Bible*, says:

> *"...it was for the terror of others in the priesthood, or who should come after, to take care that they performed their office according to the divine precepts [commands], and brought in no innovation into their service."*

Deuteronomy 12:32

Chapter 12 of the book of Deuteronomy is about worship. In this chapter, God told Israel where to worship, where not to worship, how not to worship, etc. The chapter ends with this warning: "you shall not add to it [the commands He just gave] nor take away from it." Israel was not to add anything new to the worship of God, nor omit anything that He had commanded. In worship, we must do all that God has commanded; no less, and no more.

Deuteronomy 17:3; Jeremiah 7:31, 19:5

Deuteronomy 17:2-5 shows us once again the severity with which God hates false worship. If anyone in Israel worshiped "other gods" or "the sun or moon or any of the host of heaven" (v. 3), they were to receive the death penalty (v. 5). The reason God gives is that worshiping those things is something "which I have not commanded" (v. 3). This may seem like a strange reason not to worship those things, since God had already forbidden them from doing that (Deut. 4:19). Instead of simply reminding them of the prohibition against worshiping the sun, moon, and stars, He takes another opportunity to remind them that they should only worship what, and how, He has commanded them to.

We see something similar in the book of Jeremiah. Jeremiah had the unpleasant task of warning Judah that God was going to destroy them. One of the main complaints that God had against them was their corrupted worship. Jeremiah 7:31 and 19:5 both say that the people of Judah were offering their children to false gods, and in both verses, God reminds them that this horrible practice was something that He "did not command" them to do.

So, the reason God gives for not offering their children to other gods is because that was something that He had not told them to do. But again, God had already forbidden this manner of worship (Lev. 18:21; Deut. 12:31), so God could have said, "Don't do that, because I told you not to." But instead, He says, "Don't do that, because I did not tell you to do that." I believe He was reminding them that if they had just stuck to doing what He had commanded them to do, they wouldn't be committing this sin, and they wouldn't have to worry about His judgment coming upon them. These verses show "that whatsoever is not commanded by God's word touching His service, is against His word."[8]

Genesis 1:1 — Revelation 22:21

If you have a theological disagreement with someone, it is not enough just to say that their view is wrong, and that their interpretation of certain passages is wrong. You must also give them another view to replace theirs, and give another interpretation of those passages, *and* show them passages that prove your view. So, if you disagree with my interpretation of certain passages, that's fine. I certainly could be wrong. I've tried to show that my views were held by knowledgeable and godly men from the past, but they could be wrong too. I have given a handful of passages that, I believe, prove the regulative principle. The fact that God got angry when people did things in worship that He "did not command" is enough evidence for me.

But to you, that may not be enough. If that's the case, here's my challenge to you: Please show me a handful of passages which say that we *can* make up new things to do in worship. I certainly don't have the whole Bible memorized, but in all of my reading and study, I have yet to find those passages.

---

[8] Quotation from the study note on Jer. 19:5, in the Geneva Bible (1599 edition).

Chapter 4

NEW TESTAMENT CONSIDERATIONS AND APPLICATIONS

Since most of the verses I have referenced were from the Old Testament, one might ask if the regulative principle still applies under the new covenant. And, if so, what does that look like? This chapter will attempt to answer those questions. I would summarize my view on the differences and similarities between old covenant and new covenant worship in this way: The *principles* regarding worship in the old covenant (like the regulative principle) have not changed under the new; but the *form* of worship has (e.g., we no longer sacrifice animals).

When trying to determine what things in the OT are still

in effect today, a good rule of thumb is to assume that we are still to obey the OT except when the NT tells us otherwise. The reason for this is simple: only God has the right to rescind His commands. If God gives a command in the OT, it continues to be in effect until He says it's not. While this idea is simple to understand, it's not always simple to figure out just what the new covenant repeals. Since that is a very large topic, we will only be looking at a few things that pertain to corporate worship.

One of the principles that is very clear in the OT is that worshiping God is serious business. Many in our day have the impression that God is more relaxed and not quite as uptight concerning our obedience as He was in the OT. Again, we should assume that God's attitude about the seriousness of worship has not changed unless the NT tells us it has. Furthermore, the NT shows us that God is still not to be taken lightly. God does still kill people (Acts 5:4-5, 8-10; 12:23; Rev. 2:23) and churches (Rev. 2:5); and yes, God still punishes improper worship with death. The observance of the Lord's supper is one of the elements of NT worship, and when the Corinthian Christians were doing it wrongly, God killed some of them (1 Cor. 11:27-30).

Of course, this doesn't mean that God always strikes people dead the moment they sin in worship. If God did that, then it would have been obvious to the Corinthians, and Paul wouldn't have had to tell them what was going on. God is patient and merciful, but don't take Him lightly.

As stated earlier, another principle that I believe continues on into the NT is the regulative principle. Because there is nothing in the NT that suggests that we are now free to go beyond what God has told us to do in worship, we should assume that we should still only do what He has commanded. But even though the OT is more explicit on this issue, we can still find a regulative principle mindset in the NT.

Probably the most clear NT passage on the regulative principle is found in Matt. 15:7-9 (see also Mark 7:6-7). Jesus, paraphrasing Isa. 29:13, speaks of those who "worship" according to "the commandments of men" (v. 9). And what does Jesus say about those who worship according to human inventions and innovations? He says that they are "hypocrites" (v. 7), that their "heart is far from Me" (v. 8), and that their worship is "in vain" (v. 9). Those aren't exactly compliments!

In Paul's instructions to various churches and people, we see a similar view. Being an apostle, Paul's instructions are binding; they are Scripture (2 Pet. 3:15-16), the very word of God (1 Thes. 2:13). The practices Paul gave to the church didn't come from his creativity, they came from the Lord (1 Cor. 11:23). Paul admonishes the churches to hold tightly to the traditions they had received from him (2 Thes. 2:15), and were praised when they did so (1 Cor. 11:2). Furthermore, Paul condemned those who held to the traditions of men (Col. 2:20-22; see also v. 8).

To my knowledge, none of the apostles ever told any church or individual that it was all right to invent new ways of worship. Paul's disciple, Timothy, knew how to conduct himself in the church because of what Paul *wrote* (1 Tim. 3:14-15). Likewise, we need to get our practices from what has been written by Paul and others. Though the regulative principle is taught more explicitly in the OT, it does carry over into the NT.

The *form* of worship in the OT, however, does not carry over into the new. This fact is made clear in many ways throughout the NT, with one of the most obvious examples being that we no longer sacrifice animals. There are still sacrifices under the new covenant, but these sacrifices are spiritual as opposed to physical (Heb. 13:15; 1 Pet. 2:5). Other things in the NT are of a more spiritual nature as well. For example, the "temple" of the NT is also spiritual as opposed to the physical one of the OT (1 Pet. 2:5; see also 1 Cor. 3:16; Eph. 2:19-22). More examples could be given, but hopefully it's clear that the Bible shows that the outward form of worship under the new covenant is different from the old covenant.

Because of this fact, we cannot automatically assume that we can bring OT practices into our worship services. We must do all that God requires of us, but God doesn't necessarily require the same things of us as He did of those in the OT. Of course, some elements of worship, like singing, are found in both testaments. But, if an element of worship is only found in the OT, it may be that God doesn't want us doing it anymore. I say "may," because there is some debate among those who hold to the regulative principle about what things from the OT carry over.

The worship of the old covenant must have been a feast for the senses. The sight of the brilliant colors (2 Chron. 2:7), precious stones (1 Chron. 29:2), and gold and bronze everywhere (2 Chron. 3-5); the sweet smell of incense (2 Chron. 2:4) and the sound of the singers and musicians (2 Chron.

5:12-13; 29:28; etc.) must have been quite an experience! But we don't find any of this in the NT, and that is because the outward splendor and grandeur of temple worship was a foreshadowing of the inward, spiritual splendor and grandeur of NT worship.

Many in our day try to enhance the worship experience through the use of colorful lights, smoke machines, high volume music, etc. They often justify their actions by appealing to the fact that much of OT worship did indeed excite the senses. Under the new covenant, our worship is not as showy outwardly, but it is more powerful inwardly. Don't assume that the more plain and simple worship of the NT is inferior to the worship that was held in the Jewish temple.

The idea that NT worship is to be more plain, simple, and spiritual (as opposed to physical) than OT worship also has a lot of history behind it, as these following quotes show.

John Cotton (1585-1652), pastor/theologian in colonial America:

> "...yet now in the grown age of the heires of the New Testament, such externall pompous solemnities are ceased, and no externall worship reserved, but such as holdeth forth simplicitie and gravitie..."[9]

Cotton Mather (1663-1728), pastor/theologian in colonial America; also the first historian of New England, and grandson of John Cotton:

---

9 Horton Davies, *The Worship of the American Puritans*, p. 128-129

> "...every town, for the most part can say, We have a modest and handsome house for the worship of God, not set off with gaudy, pompous, theatrical fineries, but suited unto the simplicity of Christian worship."[10]

Charles H. Spurgeon (1834-1892), English Baptist preacher. In his *The Treasury of David* (a commentary on the Psalms), he says on Psalm 4, v. 1:

> "The joy of the Jewish church was so great that they needed music to set forth the delightful feelings of their souls. Our holy mirth is none the less overflowing because we prefer to express it in a more spiritual manner, as becometh a more spiritual dispensation."

John L. Dagg (1794-1884), Southern Baptist preacher/theologian. He says:

> "Instrumental music formed a part of the temple worship; but it is nowhere commanded in the New Testament; and it is less adapted to the more spiritual service of the present dispensation."[11]

So then, what is to be done in a corporate worship service in our day? What elements of worship are acceptable? Again, there is some debate even among regulative principle adherents about what should be done in worship. A short list

---

10 Ibid., p. 14

11 John L. Dagg, D. D., *Manual of Theology, Second Part: A Treatise on Church Order* (The Southern Baptist Publication Society, 1858) reprinted by Sprinkle Publications (2012), p. 240

of the elements of worship would be:

- Scripture reading (1 Tim. 4:13)
- Preaching (2 Tim. 4:2)
- Singing (Eph. 5:19; Col. 3:16)
- Prayer (1 Tim. 2:1)
- Baptism, and…
- the Lord's Supper (Acts 2:41-42)
- Giving (of tithes and offerings; 1 Cor. 16) [12]

The largest list I have come across includes all of the above, but also adds:

- Taking Oaths & Vows (Ps. 50:14, 66:13; Deut. 29:10-13)
- Confessing the Faith (Deut. 6:13-15; Rom. 10:9)
- Pronouncing the Benediction (Num. 6:22-27; 2 Cor. 13:14)
- Exercising Church Discipline (1 Cor. 5:3-5)
- Saying a Congregational Amen (Neh. 8:6; 1 Chron. 16:36; Ps. 106: 48; we could also add 1 Cor. 14:16)
- Fasting (Matt. 6:16-17)
- Scheduling Special Days of Thanksgiving (Esth. 9:22; Ps. 107:1-3) [13]

---

[12] Both the elements of worship and their Scripture references are taken from: Scott Aniol, *Sound Worship: A Guide to Making Musical Choices in a Noisy World* (Religious Affections Ministries, 2010), p. 43. My edition references 2 Corinthians 16 as the text for taking up a collection. Since 2 Cor. 16 doesn't exist, and 1 Cor. 16 speaks of taking up a collection, I'm assuming 1 Cor. 16 is the intended reference.

[13] Elements and Scripture references taken from: Joe Morecraft, III, *How God Wants Us to Worship Him*, p. 90-96

As you can see, there are differences of opinion on what should be done in worship. Some of that is due to a difference in opinion on what is considered an element of worship. Some of the difference is due to different views on what OT elements carry over into the NT. But, in both lists, all of the elements are found in the Bible. Neither list contains extra-biblical elements.

When we compare modern worship to the commands of Scripture, it is clear that many innovations have crept into our churches. One will often find unbiblical practices such as genuflecting toward the bread & the wine, making the sign of the cross, skits or drama, interpretive dancing, puppet shows, saying the pledge of allegiance to either the American or Christian flag, altar calls, and much more. Even the time of "greeting" (handshaking) in the middle of the worship service is without biblical warrant. While there's certainly nothing wrong with shaking hands with fellow believers or guests, it isn't a biblical element of worship. Before and after the service: shake as many hands as you can! But during the service, stick to the elements of worship that are found in the Bible.

Something else that is often done in worship with no biblical warrant is dancing. Dancing is certainly found in the Bible. But there are no commands or good examples of dancing *in a worship service*. We do have many examples of God's people dancing, but these are examples of people dancing when celebrating with their families (Jdg. 11:34; Luke 15:22-25), or with the community (Jdg. 21:19-21, a feast is different from a worship service), or as a nation (Exo. 15:19-

Chapter 4: New Testament Considerations and Applications

21; 1 Sam. 18:6-7). Even David's dancing "before the LORD with all his might" did not take place in a worship service. The bringing of the ark of the LORD to the tabernacle was a time of great celebration for the nation of Israel, and celebrate they did! The tabernacle was where worship services were held, and *on the way to* the tabernacle, David danced his heart out! However, there's no mention of dancing once they reach the tabernacle (2 Sam. 6:12-19; 1 Chron. 15:25-16:2). The only example in Scripture of God's people dancing in a corporate worship service is during the infamous golden calf incident (Exo. 32:19)! Obviously, this is not an example to be followed.

But what about the Psalms? Don't the Psalms exhort us, and even command us to dance in worship? After all, Psalms 149:3 and 150:4 say to "praise His name with the dance" and "Praise Him with...dance." Aren't these commands? Not necessarily. Keep in mind that the Psalms are songs. Songs in our day and in the ancient world often used figurative language to convey certain truths. The Psalms often do the same thing (Ps. 98:8, for example). So these exhortations to dance may not be literal commands. Since the rest of the Bible doesn't contain any commands to dance in worship, that would suggest that these verses are not literal commands either.

To see this idea in a more modern song, we could look at the song *Go, Tell It on the Mountain*. This song exhorts us to "Go, tell it on the mountain, that Jesus Christ is born!" In Florida, where I live, we have no mountains. And yet, this song is still sung every Christmas. Why do we still sing this song in Florida where no one can "go tell it on a mountain?" Because everyone knows that the songwriter was not giving a literal command. He was using a figure of speech to make a point. We see this idea in one of the Psalms we looked at earlier. In Psalm 149:3 we are told to "praise His name with the dance." In that same Psalm we are told, "Let them sing aloud on their beds" and to have "a two-edged sword in their hand, To execute vengeance on the nations...To bind their kings with chains, And their nobles with fetters of iron." (vv. 5-8). I know of no one who would argue that these exhortations are to be taken as literal commands. Neither should the exhortations to dance be taken as literal commands.

But, even if these were literal commands to dance, it still isn't clear if they refer to what we do in a worship service, or some other time of celebration. Since the rest of Scripture doesn't support the idea of dancing in a worship service, it's likely that these Psalms are speaking of something else as well.

When our modern, emotion driven, visually appealing, people-pleasing worship "experiences" are compared to a purely biblical worship service, biblical worship may not seem as exciting. But in Scripture, things that look good are often not good (Col. 2:22-23; 2 Tim. 3:5), and things that look weak are often the most powerful (1 Cor. 1:21-25).

While corporate worship takes up only a small fraction of our week, what takes place during that time is important. Our attitude toward worship affects our attitude in other areas of life. If we won't be regulated by the Bible in worship, it's not likely that we will regulate other areas of life according to God's word either.

A pastor friend of mine once made a powerful statement about our view of worship and the condition of society. His point was basically that if we Christians won't allow the Bible to regulate the most important thing humans can do (worship), then what right do we have to tell unbelievers that marriage must be done according to Scripture? If we are going to make up new ways of worshiping God, then why can't the world make up new definitions of marriage?

As I said at the beginning of this booklet, the discussion of how we determine how to worship is one that the modern church needs to have. There certainly are other important debates that need to happen too, but this one shouldn't be neglected. Since fearing, glorifying, and worshiping God is the "everlasting gospel" (Rev. 14:6-7), we had better get this right.

Appendix

THE REGULATIVE PRINCIPLE FOR ALL OF LIFE?

This appendix contains a fair amount of theological "thinking out loud." I want to make a case that it is desirable to have a regulative principle mindset, not just in corporate worship, but in every area of life and society. I call this appendix theological thinking out loud for a couple of reasons:

1. Some things in Scripture are fairly easy to define and describe, but some of the general principles in Scripture are more difficult to explain precisely. The regulative principle for all of life mindset that I'm advocating is one of those principles that is hard to define precisely. And, since I'm not exactly a wordsmith, you may

not have a crystal clear understanding of what I'm describing by the time you finish this appendix. My goal in writing this appendix is simply to stimulate your thinking on how we apply God's word to every issue we will ever face.

2. While I believe that we should have a regulative principle mindset toward all of life, I'm not always sure how, or to what extent it applies to particular areas of life. So please keep in mind as you read this appendix that I'm not claiming to have figured out all the implications to this view. Nor am I claiming to give an authoritative rule to follow. Again, my hope is simply to provoke you to think about how we apply Scripture to all of life and society.

While I'm thinking out loud, let me give you something else to ponder. I'm wondering if a name change is in order. When it comes to applying the regulative principle to all of life, it is just that: a principle. But, for those of us who hold to the regulative principle of worship, isn't it more of a rule, rather than a principle? Wouldn't we say that we should *never* invent new elements of worship? Maybe we should refer to it as the *regulative rule* when applied to corporate worship, and the *regulative principle* when applied to other areas of life. I will leave any official name change to theologians who are more competent than I, but since I was thinking out loud anyway, I thought I'd mention it.

Being a Christian for about 20 years now, I've had many conversations with other Christians on a wide variety of topics. These conversations revealed that my thought process was often different from other Christians, but for many years I didn't quite know why. Another Christian and I would be discussing a particular topic, and even though we were both familiar with the passages that dealt with that topic, and we would have the same interpretation of those passages, and might even agree on the application of those passages—yet, we would still disagree on that topic! I would later learn why: they had a normative principle mindset, and I was seeing things through a regulative principle view.

For example, when discussing the issue of dating vs. courtship, we might agree on what passages spoke to that issue, and we might agree on the interpretation and application of those passages. The difference of opinion had to do with whether or not that particular application had to be followed. Their mindset was that we could follow the biblical pattern if we wanted to, but dating was just as acceptable. Why? Because the Bible doesn't say that we can't date.

The response I usually got when showing someone that the Bible advocated a certain practice was: "That's fine for you, but I'm going to do things my way because the Bible doesn't say that I can't." The focus was always on what the Bible *didn't* say. But shouldn't our focus be on what the Bible *does* say? Basing your arguments on what the Bible doesn't say is an argument from silence. Sometimes arguments from silence are legitimate, but they usually aren't the strongest. We would be much better off arguing from what the Bible does say, rather than what it doesn't.

Since the Bible has something to say about every area of life and society, we should have a regulative principle mindset toward every area of life and society. For example, God has created three covenant institutions: the family, the church, and the civil government. God has also told each of these three institutions what they are supposed to be doing. If God has not told one of these institutions to do something, then it shouldn't be doing that thing. God hasn't told the civil government to be in the welfare business, therefore, it may not do welfare. God hasn't told the family to execute criminals, therefore, the family may not put criminals to death. When an institution does things that God has not told it to do, society begins to unravel. For society to function properly, each institution needs to do what the Bible says it's supposed to do, and no more.

Another argument for the regulative principle for all of life mindset has to do with the fact that we don't have unlimited resources like time and money. We all have a limited number of hours in the day. And while there isn't a command in Scripture that forbids me from playing video games for hours and hours a day, God's word doesn't command me to do that. If I spend this much time doing things that God didn't tell me to do, then I can guarantee that I won't be doing the things that God *has* told me to do. A life spent doing meaningless things will be a meaningless life. Do you want to avoid having a meaningless life? Then just do what God has told you to do. God doesn't command meaninglessness.

This, of course, can apply to churches as well. Most modern churches spend much of their time and money doing things that aren't commanded in Scripture. These activities may not be forbidden, but a church that spends its time and money doing things that aren't commanded won't have any time or money left over to do what God has told them to do.

When I advocate for a regulative principle mindset for all of life, I'm usually met with a few objections. One objection goes something like this: "It's all right to do things that aren't in the Bible, as long as they produce good results." This idea that an activity or method is "good" if it produces good results, is called pragmatism. Pragmatism is very prevalent in the modern church. My answer to this objection is that it is much better to ask "what saith the Scriptures?" than to ask "what works?" We don't know everything; God does. We can't be certain that our man-invented ways of doing things won't produce other problems in the future. We can also be confused about whether or not something is really "working." Some things may appear to be successful, but in reality, they are not. In Matt. 7:24-27, a man wanted to build a house. That man did not build according to Jesus' words (i.e. he didn't build on the rock). But his building project was a success! He *did* build a house. His success, however, was short-lived. When the rains came, his house collapsed. He settled for what "worked" instead of doing what Jesus said, and in the long run, his success turned into failure.

In Num. 20:7-12, Moses is told to bring forth water from a rock so that the people of Israel could have something to drink. God tells Moses to "speak to the rock" (v. 8). But Moses had another method: he "struck the rock" (v. 11). God didn't tell him he *couldn't* strike the rock, but neither did He tell

Moses to do that. But Moses' method worked! Striking the rock produced the desired result! But, because Moses didn't follow the Lord's instructions, he was not allowed to lead Israel into the promised land. Pragmatism has consequences.

The second objection I often hear is that it is impossible to live life by *only* doing what God has told us to do. Because God hasn't given commands to do necessary or useful things like brushing your teeth, riding in airplanes, using the Internet, etc., no one could live their life with a regulative principle mindset. This objection is usually due to a misunderstanding of what I'm advocating. I'm not saying that we must have a specific command in Scripture before we are allowed to do something.

Remember, when I'm talking about applying the regulative principle outside of corporate worship, it is a *general principle*. Furthermore, even in corporate worship (which is more strictly regulated), there are circumstances surrounding worship which are not explicitly dealt with in Scripture. When it comes to these circumstances (see page 14), we do have more freedom to decide what we should do. So it is with the rest of life. When it comes to certain topics, the Bible gives quite a bit of instruction. The more instruction we have on a topic, the more strictly regulated that topic is. Some topics may not even be mentioned directly at all. Those topics would not be as strictly regulated.

I would mention, however, that even if a topic isn't mentioned specifically in Scripture, that doesn't mean that the Bible has nothing to say about that topic. The Bible has something to say about everything. At the very least, you can always find some general principles that apply to a particular topic. Of course, we can know things through reason, logic, experience, history, and science. Those things can help us with the details that aren't laid out explicitly in Scripture. But, our only infallible guide, and our ultimate authority, is God's word.

One advantage of having a regulative principle mindset for all of life is that it forces you to go to the Bible for guidance. It makes you re-examine how you live your life, and what you believe about the family, the church, the civil government, business, art, education, economics, etc. My confidence in the sufficiency of Scripture has increased dramatically since coming to a regulative principle mindset. Earlier, I mentioned brushing your teeth, riding in airplanes, and using the Internet. I mentioned those things because people have told me that the reason that you can't hold to a regulative principle view is because you'd have to give up those things. But would you really have to give up those things if you embraced a regulative principle mindset? Not at all.

The phrase "brush your teeth" is not in the Bible, but I believe you can still justify brushing your teeth from Scripture. God wants us to care for our bodies (1 Tim. 4:8, 5:23). The Bible also tells us that having all of your teeth is a good thing (Song of Sol. 4:2, 6:6). From this, we can conclude that God wants us caring for our teeth.

What about airplanes and the Internet? The airplane is a transportation technology. Paul and Barnabas made use of a transportation technology (Acts 13:2-4), and Jesus told His disciples to do the same (Matt. 14:22). We can conclude that

God approves the use of airplanes. The Internet is a technology that carries information from one place to another. The Bible also mentions a technology that serves the same purpose: the letter. God used this technology to carry information to His people (Col. 4:16; Rev. 2:1, 2:8, etc.). So, yes, God does approve of technologies that carry information from one place to another. Furthermore, I would argue that the invention of any technology would fall under the "dominion mandate" of Gen. 1:28. Part of subduing the earth would include using its resources to make things. I believe that Adam did this in the garden. He was told to "tend" the garden (Gen. 2:15), but God didn't give him any tools to work with. It is implied that he had to invent some.[14]

I hope it is now clear that the Bible really does have something to say about every area of life, and every issue we will ever face. Because of this, we should strive to justify our beliefs and our practices from the word of God. If we can't, then we need to repent (change our mind) and begin doing what God has told us to do in His word. While I certainly don't have everything figured out, I have come to the conviction that the instruction given to us in the Bible is far better than what even the smartest humans could invent. Things go best for us when we can justify our thoughts and deeds from Scripture. If some thing, or some method, cannot be justified from Scripture, maybe that's a clue that God has a better method or better thing for you to be doing. The closer

---

[14] For more on how to interpret and apply Scripture, please see my booklet: *Knowing God's Word, Knowing God's Will.*

you follow the Bible, the more effective your life will be for the kingdom of God, and the more God will be glorified.

"Just do what I tell you." —God

Made in the USA
San Bernardino, CA
14 June 2020